OUR NORTH AMERICAN JOURNEY

OUR NORTH AMERICAN JOURNEY

an RV adventure

by Michael and Sherleen Clivner

Our North American Journey
Copyright © 2016 by Michael and Sherleen Clivner

Editors: Regina Cornell, Kyle Weichman
Photography: Michael & Sherleen Clivner
Interior Design: Lisa DeSpain, Michael & Sherleen Clivner
Cover Design: Amy Vega, Michael & Sherleen Clivner

Indigo River Publishing
3 West Garden Street Ste. 352
Pensacola, FL 32502
www.indigoriverpublishing.com

Ordering Information:
Quantity sales: Special discounts are available on quantity purchases by corporations, associations, and others. For details, contact the publisher at the address above.
Orders by U.S. trade bookstores and wholesalers: Please contact the publisher at the address above.

Printed in the United States of America.

ISBN: 978-0-9972945-3-8
Library of Congress number: 2016953756

All rights reserved. No portion of this publication may be reproduced, stored in a retrieval system, or transmitted by any means—electronic, mechanical, photocopying, recording, or any other—except for brief quotations in printed reviews, without the prior written permission of the publisher.

With Indigo River Publishing, you can always expect great books, strong voices, and meaningful messages. Most importantly, you'll always find…words worth reading.

Preface

This is the story of our RV adventure through North America.
The goal was to see and experience all that America has to offer.

It began in April 2010 after a massive oil spill occured in the Gulf of Mexico.
It threatened the coast from Louisiana to Florida.

This was our wake-up call.
It made us realize just how fragile and temporary life as we know it is.

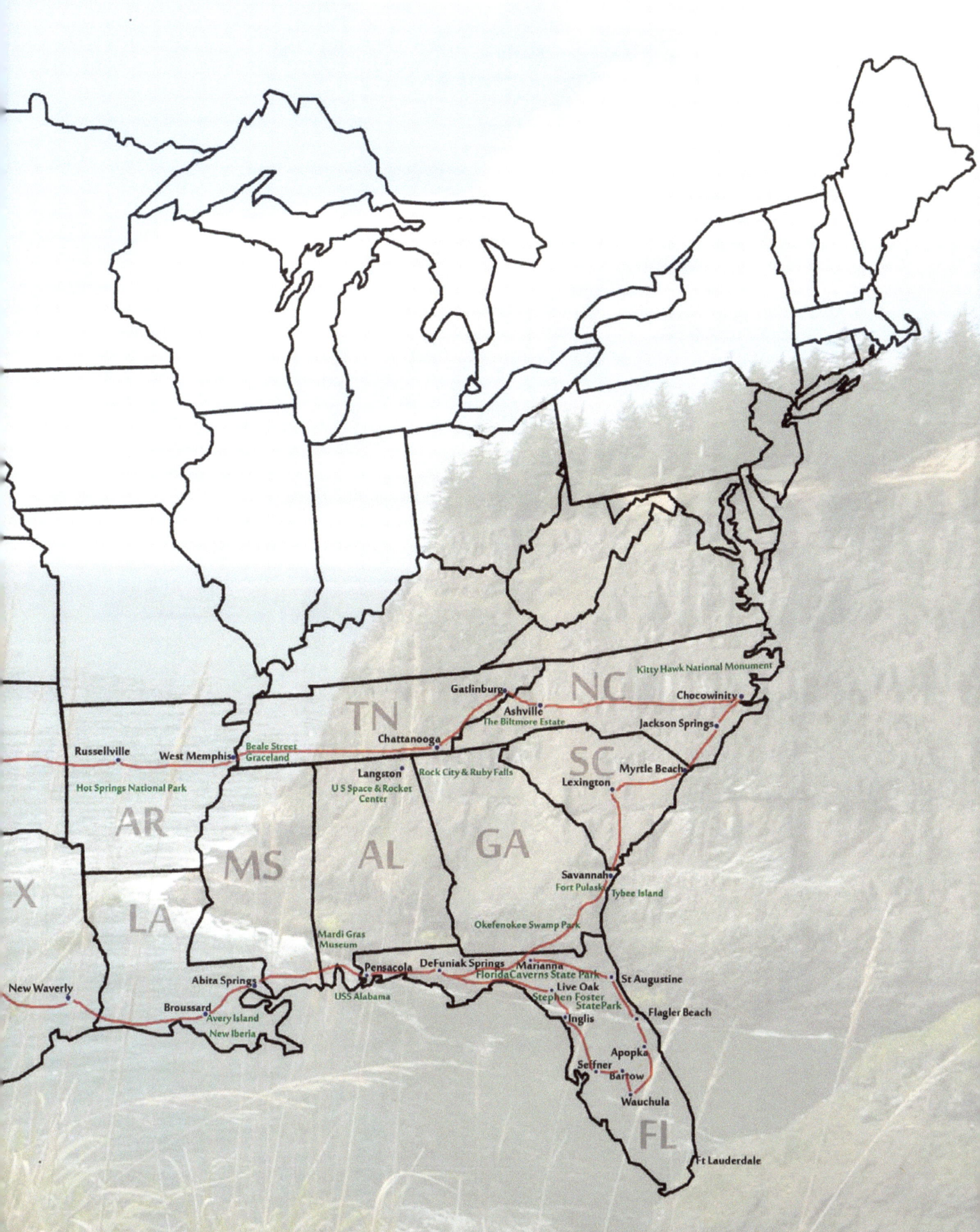

Dedicated to the memory of Dr Fred Meyer
A dear friend who will be greatly missed

He followed us avidly throughout our journey

The Planning Begins

Our goal was to start out at the end of the year. That gave us just six months to prepare for the biggest road trip of our lives.

Starting in May, our new pastime became shopping for motor homes. Michael did a lot of homework. Due to budget restraints, we were concentrating on smaller class "C" models until we found a used Class "A" which we both fell in love with. From the moment we stepped inside, we both knew that this was the one for us. This turned out to be the right choice, since we ended up living in it for the next three years.

On July 31st, 2010 we signed the papers and became the proud owners of a 33 foot Class "A" motor home. Although it was an older model, built in 1997, it had low mileage and the previous owners took extremely good care of it. Since we were not planning on actually starting our journey for a few months, we had time for a few minor renovations. The staff at Camping World, in Gulf Breeze, FL, where we bought it was great. They allowed us to keep it parked on their back lot for six months at no charge as we prepared for our journey.

A trip of this caliber takes a lot of preparation and planning. You don't just get behind the wheel and go. We wanted our trip to be as unregimented as possible, but to do so required a lot of advance planning. We would also be travelling with a bird, a Quaker parrot, named Sam, which we inherited when Sherleen's Mom passed away in 2001. Thank goodness he was a good little traveler. So here we were, just the three of us, setting off on this incredible journey. Some would call us crazy, but we prefer the word adventurous.

The first thing we did was buy a large wall map of North America, and with the use of colored pins, started marking all of the places of interest. After that, it was just a matter of connecting the dots. Our goal was to be able to see all of the places on our list in the most fuel efficient and comfortable manner as possible. Our vision was quickly becoming reality.

Next, we began accumulating various electronic items which we wanted for our trip. We bought an MP3 player to download our favorite music to take with us. One of the most useful items was our Garmin navigation device, which for the most part was a life-saver, but did on rare occasions manage to get us lost. Another item which proved to be invaluable was a portable wireless device which we bought through our cell phone provider. This enabled us to stay connected while on the road, even in the most remote areas. We picked up a pair of two-way radios for communication when we were separated in a park. They also came in handy when backing into a camp site.

One thing we discovered was that you "must" have a valid address if you live in the United States. We set ours up with one of the many mail-forwarding companies and periodically would call them and have them send everything to us. We eliminated most of our mail by setting up "E" billing and paying bills via our bank's online bill-pay.

By the end of the year, we were ready to get started. We had taken the motor home out for a test weekend drive to a nearby RV resort, sort of a shake-down trip. We had all of our household belongings safely stored away in a mini-warehouse unit. We had quit our jobs and said good-bye to our friends. It was now time for us to hit the road for real.

By August, we had made it across the country and up the west coast, when we decided to stay in Oregon for while before starting our return trip eastbound. Since our grandson lived nearby, this also gave us the opportunity to spend more time with him, which was our main reason for selecting this area for our temporary home. We enjoyed the northwest and visited all of the local sights, of which there were many.

After two years of staying in one place, it was time to continue our journey. Although it was hard to leave our grandson behind, we wanted to get started in time to miss the winter weather while on the road. The second half of our journey did not take as much preparation as the first. We just unplugged and drove away.

Before we left Oregon, we did do some major mechanical maintenance on our motor home. We also did a little remodeling, which included new carpet, a new sofa and new upholstery.

Although we had a much longer and interesting route planned for the return trip, the 2013 government shutdown prevented us from visiting the majority of the places we had wanted to see. We saw what we could before heading south back to Florida. Guess our North American Journey will have "To Be Continued".

FLORIDA

The Suwannee River

Pensacola Beach

Our journey began in what is referred to as the "panhandle" of Florida, in the small town of Pensacola, where we had lived for the past two years. It is rich in history, tradition and natural beauty.

Each spring you will find the beaches in full bloom with sea daisies as well as sea oats.

The beaches are the habitat for many birds and is also the nesting grounds for sea turtles.

Many of the sand dunes are blocked off to avoid trespassing, which could endanger the balance this delicate environment.

Pensacola is also the home of the world famous Blue Angels. It is a common sight to see them shooting across the skies high above the city and nearby beaches. Twice a year they host a spectacular air show for the community to show off their amazing aeronautical skills.

The Pensacola lighthouse is located on the Naval Air Station which is more commonly referred to as simply "NAS". It dates back to 1859 and is still in operation to aide navigation into the bay.
Legend has it that it is haunted. You can check it out for yourself by taking one of the many tours offered to the public.

Being the middle of winter when we began our journey, we thought it wise to stay south before actually starting our trek westward. This also gave us the opportunity to explore Florida and to become more accustomed to life on the road.

In the beginning we tried to keep our travel days short, as it takes longer to travel by motor home than by car. Our average speed was about 60 mph. Driving a motor home is much more intense than driving a car. Our overall length was more than 54 feet, which made sudden stops difficult. You must always be watching for merging and stopping traffic around you.

Our first stop was at DeFuniak Springs. Although there were no actual "springs" there, we did manage to camp next to the very peaceful Holley King Lake.

Our next and also one of our favorite stops was in Live Oak, FL, at the Spirit of the Suwannee Music Park. We were surrounded by beautiful moss covered trees along the famous Suwannee River. Our timing allowed us to celebrate "Stephen Foster Day" at the Stephen Foster Folk Culture Center in White Springs, FL.

Every year students compete for the titles of "Stephen" and "Jeanie" Foster. We happened to be lucky enough to see this year's couple as they performed songs composed by the famous songwriter. It was delightful to see young people with such appreciation for the art and music of a bygone era. All of this takes place in a town of only 800 people. How commendable to see a town so enriched by and devoted to their past. As we prepare to leave, we too would take away a greater appreciation for this area than we could ever have imagined.

We also have learned a great deal about a man called Stephen Foster. By the way, he never saw the river which he made famous in his song.

Homosassa Springs was our next destination. As luck would have it, at the time we were there the water level was unusually low, thus preventing the migrating manatees easy access to the park. We still enjoyed ourselves and did see a few manatees along with other species of Florida plants and wildlife.

At our campground in Inglis, FL, we were treated to an amazing Bluegrass concert by a local family band. It was refreshing to see such talent by some of the younger members. They entertained us for over two hours. Instead of paying for tickets, the park manager simply passed around a hat at the end of the show. We have been truly impressed by the music in this part of the country. It really depicts the heritage of the area.

In addition to the manatees, this portion of the trip was to also visit family in the area and to coincide with one of the largest RV shows in the country, which is held early in the year outside of Tampa. This show is a must for anyone interested in RVing. There are booths full of helpful information, every type of merchandise available and of course more models of RVs than you could ever imagine in one place, we were overwhelmed to say the least. We even checked out one that was selling for 1.5 million dollars. A little out of our budget, but looking is free.

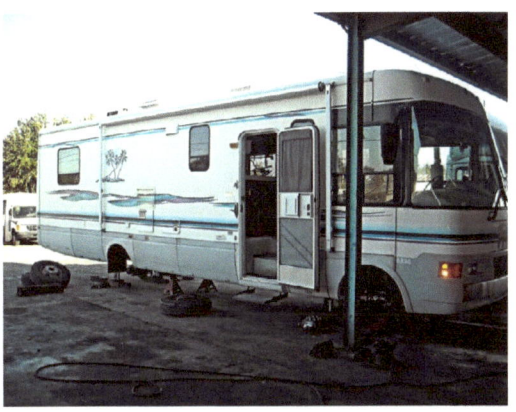

After a couple of days spent at the repair shop and with our new tires and brakes, we resumed our journey southward toward Wauchula, FL and the lovely Peace River.

As indicated by its name, Peace River was just that. This would be our most southern stop before turning north to begin the real trip.

Blue Spring

Homosassa Springs

A trip through Florida would not be complete without a stop at the Kennedy Space Center. We tried to delay our trip long enough to see the space shuttle Discovery's final launch. But due to several delays, it did not go up until February 24th, 2011. Sadly we could not stick around until then.

Apollo Saturn second stage engines

Launch Pad 39A, where the Space Shuttle Discovery sits awaiting its final mission

Although we are not particularly big racing fans, we were very impressed by just the massiveness of the Daytona Speedway. Visiting it on a non-race day is quite a surreal experience.

Mountains in Florida? Not exactly, but Mount Dora is a quaint New England style village dating back to the 1800's. It is a mecca for antique shoppers and even boasts its own lighthouse on Lake Dora.

Not far from Daytona is the city of St. Augustine, FL. It was established in 1565 and is the oldest permanent European settlement in the continental United States.

The Castillo de San Marco is a monument to Spanish engineering and artistry. Though the National Park Service will not give them real cannonballs, you will still find the soldiers defending themselves against the British.

St. Augustine, FL is home to the famous "Fountain of Youth" and was also the first capital of the Florida territory. Much of the Spanish influence is still intact throughout the city.

After St. Augustine, we returned to our favorite Spirit of the Suwannee Park to spend our last few days in Florida relaxing.

Our last stop in Florida was the Florida Caverns State Park in Marianna, FL. It was our first experience camping in a State Park and we found it absolutely wonderful. We camped beneath tall pines. It was not yet the busy time of the year and we practically had the place all to ourselves. We did a lot of bike riding and hiking.

Far beneath the surface are the caverns themselves. They are the only caverns in Florida that are open to the public.

Not all of the mysteries and beauty lie underground. We discovered "cypress knees". They look like broken off little trees, but are, in reality, extensions of the larger cypress trees that reach up above the surface in order to provide air to the original trees, which sometimes live with their lower trunks completely submerged in water.

LOUISIANA

Cemetary Statue in Mandeville

Shadows on the Teche

The McIlhenny Company Building

Some of the tastes and sights of New Orleans

We stayed in Abita Springs, LA, home of the beer with the same name. New Orleans was just across Lake Pontchartrain, and we happened to be there during Mardi Gras. So why not check it out?

In order to cross the lake into New Orleans we took the Lake Pontchartrain Causeway Bridge. At almost 24 miles in length, it is the longest bridge in the world.

St. Louis Cathedral towers above the trees at Jackson Square

Mardi Gras transforms Bourbon Street into one big party as both young and old celebrate the season. There are parades on every street and music on every corner.

"Laissez les bons temps rouler" as they say down there.

New Iberia, LA predates the Civil War and is home to America's oldest rice mill and Avery Island, where the famous Tabasco sauce is manufactured

This entire area is very rich in the heritage of the long-suffering Cajuns. Their zest for life is so incredible, given all of the suffering that they have endured. Of all the places that we visited, this area was truly one of the most moving and inspiring.

While in New Iberia, we were able to visit one of the most famous historic homes in the area, known as "Shadows-on-the-Teche", and dates back to the early 1800s.

The Tabasco Factory is located on Avery Island, which is not really an island, but in fact, a salt dome. The salt is mined as part of their production process.

Also on Avery Island is "Jungle Gardens", a 170 acre park, also owned by the Mcilhenny family. One of the many features of this park is "Bird City", which is a sanctuary for migrating egrets, started back in the 1890s with just eight birds. Today it is home to thousands of egrets.

Just months after the Gulf Oil Spill, fishing boats were packed in like sardines at the docks at Intracoastal City. It was too expensive to head out in exhange for the small amount of harvest. The fishermen were taking this opportunity to repair and maintain their boats in preparation for when they could resume their livelihood.

The Konriko Rice Mill, circa 1912, still operates with the original machinery. The only modern additions are the two packaging machines. It is indeed, a working antique.

In the Jungle Gardens

The Superstition Mountains

THE SOUTHWEST

It is impossible to travel across this great nation of ours without going through at least some part of Texas. One of the places that we stopped was Glen Rose, just south of Dallas. This is Texas hill country and was also where we got to see the first signs of spring appear.

Camping along the Brazos River was not quite like the Suwannee, but it had its own style, and as it greened up, its own beauty as well.

While there, we met up with friends, also RVers, whom we had met back in Alabama when we were just starting our journey. We had a lot of catching up to do.

The Brazos River

Located along the Paluxy River near Glen Rose is Dinosaur Valley State Park, where you can walk among fossilized dinosaur tracks from over 113 million years ago.

Another one of our favorite cities in New Mexico is Taos. Having visited it many times during ski season, it was nice to just spend the day exploring the many galleries, shops, and restaurants.

While there we found a wonderful little oil painting by a local artist whom we met. It just happened to be "motor home size", so of course we had to find the "spot" which inspired the painting. Scenes such as this can be found all around the city.

Hollyhocks can also be seen blooming everywhere and seem to be favored by artists, as they are featured in many works of art.

Nestled in a scenic valley in southern New Mexico is the town of Ruidoso, best known for its horse racing.

While exploring town, we discovered this charming old grist mill which serves as a tourist information center today.

Our friends that we met up with in Glen Rose earlier own an RV Park in Ruidoso. It is called "Along the River RV Park" and they invited us to stay with them for a while.

It was really hard to leave such a peaceful place and such good friends, but it was time to move on.

We have always loved New Mexico, and especially Santa Fe. It was great to be back.

Founded in 1608, it is one of our oldest cities and is the oldest capital city in the United States.

Entering the famous Plaza via the Old Santa Fe Trail puts you right in the heart of the city.

The La Fonda is a grand old hotel and one of the cornerstones of the Plaza. Throughout the interior you can see the true Spanish style of architecture and decor.

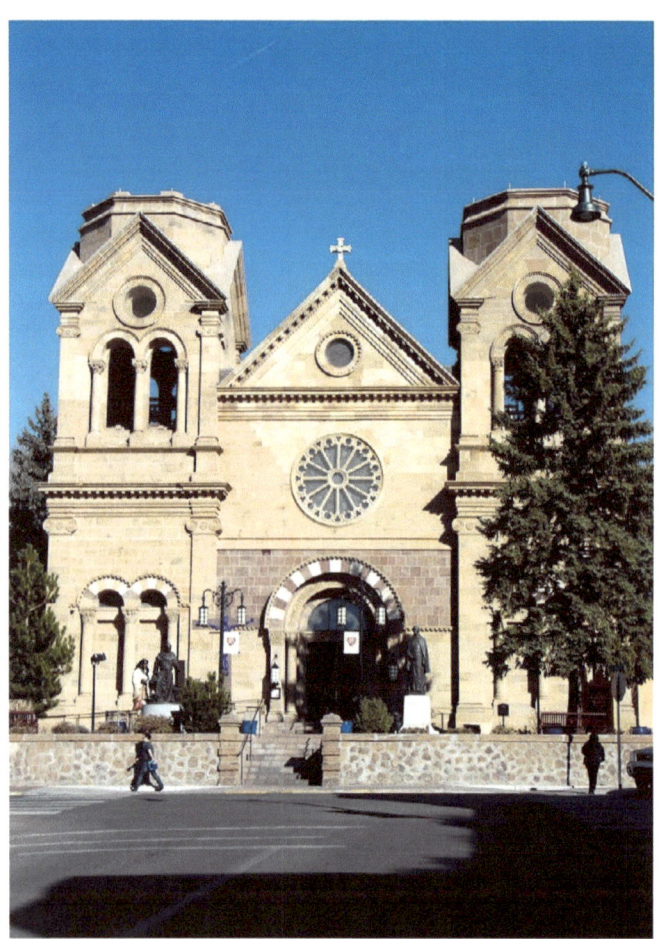

The Cathedral of St. Francis, at the end of San Francisco Street is still missing its two towers. Why they were never finished still remains a mystery.

Once again our timing was perfect. We managed to arrive just at the end of ski season. We were able to get a day of delightful spring skiing in at the Santa Fe Ski Basin before moving on.

This is the Chapel of Loretto in downtown Santa Fe. Inside is the Miraculous Staircase built in the 1800s by a mysterious stranger. Many believe that St. Joseph, himself, was responsible for this incredible feat of woodworking.

Trinity Site, located on the White Sands Missile Range in southern New Mexico is where the first explosion of the atomic bomb took place. At the time that we were there, it was only open to the public twice a year, the first Saturday in April and the first Saturday in October. We were lucky to have been nearby for the April date. We have recently learned that due to fiscal constraints, the government has now reduced the event to just once a year, in April.

Trinity Site is, as it should be, pretty desolate. Ringed by mountains, it is a natural flat bowl which made it the perfect place for the culmination of Robert Oppenheimer's Manhattan Project.

Work on the site began in the fall of 1944 and ended with the first atomic explosion on July 16th, 1945. About two miles from the site was a lone ranch house owned by George McDonald. Here the plutonium core was assembled. It was not exactly the clean room environment you would expect. The core was put together in the master bedroom. Duct tape and plastic sheeting provided the "clean" part. The core was then transported to the "Gadget", as it was called, located on a tower 100 feet above the desert floor. People actually handled this thing! Oppenheimer and his associates retreated to wood and concrete bunkers only 10,000 yards from the tower to observe the test. They did not know if it was going to work, fail or burn up the entire atmosphere. Well, it worked. It lit up and shook the entire state of New Mexico and then some. Oppenheimer's comment was a quote from the Bhagavad Gita: "I am become death, the shatterer of worlds!"

Today it is a very quiet and solemn place. All of the buildings and support structures are gone except for the ranch house. Scattered around the site are remnants of the fused desert floor created by the fireball that registered 14,710 degree F. This stuff is called Trinitite and is still radioactive. Needless to say they do not advise taking home souvenirs. A simple lava stone obelisk with a bronze plaque commemorating the event marks ground zero. There is more to think about here than to see.

One of our most interesting stops was Meteor Crater, located in northern Arizona. The crater was created over 50,000 years ago when a chunk of metal and rock about 150 feet across hit the desert floor. Burning up on impact it left behind this 700 feet deep and 4,000 feet wide hole in the ground.

Meteor Crater is the best preserved impact site on earth and was used by NASA as a training site for the Apollo astronauts.

Sunset over the Meteor Crater

Could this have been the inspiration for the Arizona State Flag?

The Holsinger Meteorite is the largest discovered fragment of the meteor responsible for creating Meteor Crater.

Pinnacle Peak is a local landmark of the Arizona desert and is most beautiful when the spring wildflowers are in bloom.

Lost Dutchman State Park is located on the backside of the Superstition Mountains. It is a favorite for hikers and horseback riders.

The legendary Lost Dutchman's Mine is the most famous lost mine in American history. Many believe that it really exists hidden deep within the Superstition Mountains.

Looking at the Superstition Mountains

The Salt River from under the Route 60 bridge

Our stop in Las Vegas was to visit with family. Although it was just a short stop, we did manage to see a couple of shows. We are not big gamblers, but we did enjoy the warmth and sunshine. We feel that Las Vegas is most definitely prettiest at night when it is all lit up.

The bridge under construction

Crossing from Nevada to Arizona gave us the opportunity to check out the new bridge that had just been completed in 2010. It is the world's highest concrete arch bridge and stands 804 feet above the Colorado River which separates the two states. Although we really appreciate the new and quicker bridge, we still like the older route with its art deco design, which takes your across the top of the actual dam itself. We also recommend the Hoover Dam tour. It is well worth the time and expense.

Our first stop in California was at Palm Springs. We have always enjoyed this desert oasis, having made many weekend trips there when we lived in Arizona. We usually stayed at our time-share in Palm Desert. This was our first time in our motor home. We were also able to relax at the pool and eat at all of our favorite restaurants. Again we met up with more family before continuing to the coast.

Palm Springs is where the desert ends and the California mountains begin, as we would soon discover. We also discovered that the best route is not always the shortest route as noted on the map. If you are travelling by motor home, we would not recommend taking HWY 74 from Palm Springs to San Diego (as thrilling as it might be). We managed to burn up our new brakes and again found ourselves seeking the assistance of mechanics.

After our adventurous drive over the mountains it was nice to just relax in a quiet spot closer to sea-level. We stayed in Ramona, which is about 40 miles north of San Diego. When not hanging out at the local garage getting our brakes repaired we hiked around the hills surrounding our park. This was also another opportunity for us to visit with family and friends in the San Diego area.

We visited the Hotel Del Coronado on Coronado Island, just across the bay from downtown San Diego. When this famous landmark opened in 1888, it was the world's largest luxury hotel and has hosted presidents, celebrities and even royalty. In the 1920's it was the place of choice for those wanting to see and to be seen.

In 1904 Thomas Edison oversaw the world's first electrically lit Christmas tree which was set up on the lawn of the hotel.

Sunset on Mission Beach

The beach on Coronado Island

Yosemite National Park was another one of our favorite places. Our RV park was just south of the park and only a short drive to the entrance, allowing us to make day trips in and out of the park. From the south gate it is about 35 miles into the heart of the park, which only builds up your expectations. You enter via a tunnel cut into the rock. As you approach the end of the tunnel, the valley suddenly appears in all its glory. Just on the other side of the tunnel is an overlook where you get your first view of the park. From this vantage point you can see El Capitan, Half Dome, North Dome and Bridal Veil Falls.

Our first stop was Mirror Lake, which only appears from late spring to early summer. Crystal clear, it becomes a reflecting pool at the foot of Half Dome and North Dome. Hiking above the lake took us through meadows, forests and streams, nature's eye candy.

We next took the trail to Vernal Falls, which is towards the east end of the park. To get there we passed through the valley that contains Nevada Falls, which helps Vernal Falls feed the Merced River. This was quite a climb, but oh so worth it!

Below Vernal Falls

Nevada Falls

Then it is back on our bikes to Yosemite Falls, which drops about 1400 feet in two sections, upper and lower.

Yosemite sets the standard for waterfalls everywhere. Throughout the rest of our trip we never saw another waterfall that could compare to the ones in Yosemite.

As the sun sets, moisture at the top of El Capitan creates a waterfall of white fire. This amazing event can only be seen for a limited time once a year, when the snow is melting.

Just past the south entrance to Yosemite there is a turnoff to a quiet little area called the Mariposa Grove of Giant Sequoias, the largest living things known to man. It is quiet in sound only. Visually it explodes in visions of giant wonder. These trees are beyond comparison to any we have seen anywhere in the world.

Even though it was May, there was still a lot of snow on the ground, especially at the higher elevations. We hiked above the snow line to get some of these shots and found ourselves totally alone in this forest. We passed the old "Tunnel Tree" which collapsed in 1969. How sad to see it broken and lying on its side. The rest of the hike made us realize just how little we humans are just by looking around us.

The tree Sherleen is standing in is called the "Telescope Tree" because it is hollow all the way to the top. As you lean back into it and look up you can see the sky. Truly amazing.

Big Tree, Little Me

This should give you an idea of the size of these things (*if you can even find me in the photo*).

From Yosemite we made a detour west in order to visit more family and friends. We stayed in the central California area known as the delta region, which is one of the richest farming areas in the country. There are wonderful fruit and vegetable stands along every highway and road. It was indeed a treat.

We have friends in the Napa area and were invited to spend some time with them. We visited many of the world famous wineries of the area, including Stags Leap and the Rubicon Estate Winery. The latter of which is owned by the Francis Ford Coppola family. It is a magnificent mansion and winery surrounded by vineyards and the valley itself.

Since it was spring, the grapes were just beginning to form. Oh, how great it would be to come back in the fall at harvest time.

Shasta Lake, with aqua blue, tree-lined waters and surrounded by spectacular mountains has to be one of the most beautiful lakes in the country, if not the world. No wonder it is the house boat capital of the western world. We were even invited aboard one and given a tour by the owner. Perhaps we should trade our motor home in for a houseboat?

We also visited the Lake Shasta Caverns. Although the caverns were quite nice, we enjoyed the boat ride across the lake even more.

The lake was created by Shasta Dam, begun in 1937 right after Hoover Dam was completed. Frank Crowe was the Chief Engineer on both projects. He learned so much from building Hoover Dam that he completed Shasta more than two years ahead of schedule. Although not as tall as Hoover Dam, Shasta Dam is larger in mass. The dam is also lacking in the artistry of Hoover Dam and its wonderful Art Deco forms, but the view of the Sacramento River Valley below and the tree-lined mountains around the lake above more than make up for it.

Mt. Shasta, which played hide and seek with us the whole time we were there, is quite a sight when it does finally appear out of the clouds. Snow covered rather than snow capped, it dominates the entire area.

This majestic mountain is actually a volcano. The last significant eruption may have occurred as recently as two centuries ago.

We got as close as we could until stopped by the previous winter's heavy snowfall. It is hard to believe that there could be this much snow in mid-May.

OREGON

Cape Meares

The Wooden Shoe Tulip Farm, Woodburn

In our opinion, the Oregon Coast is one of the most spectacular coastlines in the world. It is so alive. Our campsite was just outside of Pacific City, overlooking Nestucca Bay on the North Central Coast. A short walk across the road was the Pacific Ocean. Every bay and cove had something new to visually enjoy, with each one seeming more spectacular than the last. The waters are pristine, the forests and mountains lush, and the sky deep blue with a wonderful variety of clouds. We did amazing hikes with scenic vistas looking out to the vast Pacific Ocean.

Our first night there we were treated to a magnificent sunset which set the standard for our visit to this beautiful coast.

One of the many scenic stops along Highway 101 is Boiler Bay State Park. Based on the view, one might think that this spot was named for the turbulent waters below the cliffs. But that is not the case. It actually gets its name from a shipwreck. In 1910, the J. Marhoffer, a 175-foot steam schooner caught fire. In the explosion, parts of the ship ended up on the shore here. During low tides part of the ship's boiler is still visible, thus the name "Boiler Bay".

Cape Meares Lighthouse is no longer active, but is open to the public for tours.

There are a total of eleven lighthouses along the Oregon coast, each one unique in its own design and history.

Cape Foulweather is just one of the many capes dotting the Oregon coast. Named by Captain James Cook, it was the first promontory on the northwest coast he saw while on his third voyage around the world. He named it Cape Foulweather because of the weather he encountered shortly afterwards.

There are dozens of spectacular lookouts such as this up and down the Oregon coast. We tried to see them all. Needless to say, we made a lot of stops.

All of these lookouts are great for whale watching as well.

Haystack Rock is a 235 foot sea stack and local landmark for the town of Cannon Beach. It can be reached on foot during low tide.

Cannon Beach is Oregon's answer to California's Carmel and is a popular vacation spot for locals and tourists.

The historic town of Astoria is located in the northwestern corner of the state at the mouth of the mighty Columbia River. Astoria is the oldest settlement west of the Rockies, dating back to 1805 and the Lewis and Clark expedition. We happened to be there during their bicentennial celebration. This historic occasion was kicked off with the grand entrance of two tall ships, The Lady Washington and the Hawaiian Chieftain.

The Astoria Column is a 125-foot tower overlooking the Columbia River. It was built in 1926 with financing from the Great Northern Railway and Vincent Astor, the great-grandson of John Jacob Astor. There is a 164-step spiral staircase ascending to an observation deck at the top. Well worth the climb.

Astoria has been the setting for several movies. One of the most well-known was "The Goonies", filmed in 1985.

We discovered that not all covered bridges are in Madison County. Seems that Lane County in Oregon is also famous for them.

The 105 foot long Dorena Bridge (above) was built in 1949.

The Chambers Railroad Bridge (right) is the only remaining covered railroad bridge in Oregon and perhaps the only one west of the Mississippi River. It was in use from 1925 to 1951. After many years of neglect and non use, the bridge was reconstructed by the city of Cottage Grove and reopened to the public in 2011.

Not all of the bridges are covered. Just east of the coastal city of Florence, we saw this unusual bridge. Don't know who lives in the bridge-top house, or why for that matter, but still found it interesting.

Below is the Yaquina Bridge in Newport:

Following page: The Siuslaw Bridge in Florence which was added to the National Register of Historic Places on Aug 5, 2005.

The Siuslaw River Bridge in Florence, OR was added to the National Register of Historic Places on August 5, 2005.

The Oregon landscape is ablaze with the rich colors of fall. It was our first time seeing such a scene in many years and we were totally enamored.

We were so happy that spring had finally arrived. Well, maybe in the rest of the country, but not in Oregon. We woke up one March morning to about five or six inches of snow everywhere. Just a note, that much snow on the awning of our motor home was not a good thing. On the other hand, there is a certain beauty to this monochrome kind of day.

Spring did finally arrive to the Willamette Valley, and with it a new palette of green. None more beautiful than the many vineyards scattered throughout the area. The surrounding hills became a patchwork quilt in a multitude of shades and designs.

Another rite of spring in Oregon is the annual Tulip Festival at the Wooden Shoe Tulip Farm just outside of Woodburn, Oregon. Planting began in 1974 and has been going strong ever since. This festival draws visitors from all over the world. It is one of the largest displays of tulips in the country. The fields seem to go on forever with every imaginable color and texture.

South of Florence is the Oregon Dunes National Recreation Area. These dunes cover over 40 miles of the Oregon coast, stretching all the way down to North Bend. Although not the pristine white of Florida's Emerald Coast, this is a vast sea of ultra-fine cream to caramel colored sand.

This area is as bleak as it is beautiful and is a paradise for dune buggies. The wonderful thing is how the Pacific winds keep the dunes smooth and clean. It reminded us of Utah powder snow on the first run of the day.

Our next stop was the Umpqua Lighthouse and the still active Coast Guard Station there. The lighthouse is located south of Winchester Bay and overlooks the Umpqua Tribal oyster beds.

Travel southwest about 16 miles from Coos Bay past Sunset Bay and the small seaport village of Charleston until the road ends and you will find yourself at Cape Arago State Park. Cape Arago is a scenic headland jutting into the Pacific Ocean and it is rumored that Sir Francis Drake anchored here in June of 1579.

The coast here is dramatic and ever-changing and always a feast for the eyes. This is another favorite spot for whale watching.

Up until 2006 the Cape Arago Lighthouse at Gregory Point was still helping vessels find their way home.

A view of the Columbia River Gorge as seen from Crown Point, not too far from Portland, OR. The Columbia River Gorge is a canyon more than 80 miles long, cutting through the Cascades separating Oregon and Washington. It was formed from Ice Age floods and is flanked by volcanic cliffs, some rising as high as 3000 feet.

Crater Lake is Oregon's only National Park. Due to snow and road conditions we were unable to get there when we first arrived in Oregon in the spring, so we decided that it would be a good place to begin the second half of our journey. Again we found our timing not the best. Due to forest fires to the west, yet again we were unable to see this mysterious lake, which seemed to act like a funnel drawing in the surrounding smoke.

The lake was formed when Mt. Mazama, an active volcano at the time, erupted some 7700 years ago. Rather than blowing its top, it collapsed within itself, creating a caldera 6 miles wide and over 1900 feet deep. Subsequent magma buildups and flows sealed the bottom and created Wizard Island, which can be seen in the middle of the lake. Wizard Island is a volcanic dome, essentially a volcano within a volcano. Over centuries of rain and snowfall, the crater filled with some of the purest water on the continent. There are no rivers, streams or runoff to add sediment to the mix. This purity is what gives the lake its vibrant blue color.

Miraculously by our second day, the smoke had lifted and right before our eyes this spectacular natural wonder appeared.

Southeast of the lake we discovered "The Pinnacles" which are the remains of volcanic vents that rose up through an ash layer leaving these "Fossil" Fumaroles behind.

North of Crater Lake and just south of Bend, is the Newberry Volcanic National Monument. At the north end is Lava Butte, a cinder cone dating back to over 7000 years ago. You must take a corkscrew drive up in order to reach the top. Once there, we hiked around the rim, taking in the panoramic views, which included Mt. Bachelor and the Three Sisters, two local year round favorite areas.

Heading south, we hiked in "The Lava Cast Forest", where a lava flow passed through over 6000 years ago. Twisted limbs and stone-shaped holes from where trees once stood is all that remain of this ancient forest. These tree molds were formed when the molten lava engulfed the trees and cooled around them. This is a peaceful, somber place today. It is hard to imagine the devastation that took place here so long ago.

The Big Obsidian Flow is one of the most popular and amazing features of the Newberry Volcanic National Monument. The area is still geologically active, with the last eruption occurring just a little over 1300 years ago. We hiked up to the top of this mountain of glass, which was breathtakingly beautiful as the sunlight reflected off of the black rocks.

From the top we were able to see Paulina Lake, one of the twin crater lakes located in Newberry Crater.

Paulina Falls, dropping 80 feet onto a bed of rocks, lies just below the peak and is fed by Lake Paulina, the larger of the two lakes.

New life emerges from devastation.

It took us two attempts to actually see Mt. St. Helens. It becomes enshrouded by clouds and completely disappears. We will never forget when we gazed upon it for the first time. It was totally surreal. As you look at what remains of the mountain, you can almost feel the earth move beneath you. You struggle to envision what it was like on that fateful day in May of 1980, but the immensity of the eruption that took off an entire side of the mountain is almost beyond comprehension. Try to imagine over 1000 feet of mountain top turning into ash and rubble in an instant. The entire northwest face collapsed and headed down the Toutle River. When the ash flow reached the Columbia River it made a slight change in navigation. The river went from 600 feet wide and 40 feet deep to 200 feet wide and 14 feet deep all in a day or so, blocking all shipping for months. The blast area was nine miles wide and took out everything in its path, including 59 people and around 60,000 acres of forests. Most of the forests have since been replanted.

Our closest viewpoint was at Johnston Ridge, five miles from the crater. A young volcanologist named David Johnston had the misfortune of being on monitor duty that fateful day. What a terrifying sight he must have seen just before the mountai took him. He was never found, but the observatory and visitor center is aptly named in his honor.

Preceeding page: The view from Desolation Area

From our RV park on a clear day we could see both Mt. St. Helens and Mt. Rainier at the same time.

Mt. Rainier is another majestic mountain with an elusive spirit. So seeing it also had its challenges. We were in the parking lot of the visitor center looking at a cloud bank, where the mountain should have been, when all of a sudden the clouds started to part like some theatrical grand curtain. Everyone there stood transfixed, watching this view unfold. Mt. Rainier appeared and within an hour was gone. That was a rather well timed afternoon.

Mt. Rainier is over 14,000 feet high and is the tallest mountain in the continental United States.

Following: Culditz Glacier

We again find ourselves camped in a dense forest of tall trees. This time we are on the outskirts of the Olympic National Park, just north of Hoodsport, WA. The Olympic Mountain Range was created by gentle uplifts rather than the volcanic violence which created the Cascades to the southeast. Here rain forests abound and grow right to the northwestern shores. The coast is somewhat less dramatic than Oregon's, but of equal beauty. Helped by the winter's massive snowfall, rivers and streams were everywhere. Snow still covered most of the mountain tops throughout the area.

This area, known as "Staircase", was named for the way the Skokomish River flows over some very step-like rock formations. In order to get there we hiked through a rich and steamy rain forest. In some areas we were walking on a carpet of bright moss. The rain forests of the Olympic Mountain Range receive moisture almost every day of the year.

We drove into Bremerton and took the ferry over to Seattle for the day. What a great way to travel. Because of all the military ship traffic they don't have many bridges, so they use ferries to cross back and forth across Puget Sound. Don't think we have ever seen so many coffee shops in any one place before. From Pike Street Market to the Space Needle, Seattle is a wonderful place. It is amazing what throwing a few fish around can do for one's business.

The Seattle Space Needle is a landmark for the northwest. Built for the 1962 World's Fair, it features an observation deck and a revolving restaurant.

Welcome to Cape Flattery.

The northwest coast of the Olympic Peninsula is full of breathtakingly beautiful coves and lookouts, such as this one that we saw while on our way to Cape Flattery. If you look closely enough you may even see a puffin or two nesting on the rocky outcroppings.

Cape Flattery is the northwestern tip of the lower 48 states. In order to reach this coastal tip of the country we had to walk through a forest that was right out of Middle Earth. It felt as if the trees could come to life at any moment. Although fascinating, it was a bit eerie.

In 1778 James Cook was so flattered by the harbor when he saw it that he named it Cape Flattery.

North and west along the Strait of Juan de Fuca, which separates Washington from Canada's Vancouver Island, is Dungeness Bay. There you will find Dungeness Spit, a 5.5 mile natural sand spit, the longest in the world.

Just south of Dungeness Bay and inland is Hurricane Ridge. It is so named because the winter storms at the top can reach 100 mph. On a clear day it is possible to see the northern Cascades across Puget Sound.

Still on the Olympic Peninsula, but a little closer to sea level is Lake Crescent. Its amazing blue color is due to the lack of nitrogen, which inhibits the growth of algae.

It was time to leave the Olympic Peninsula and head inland to the Cascade Mountain Range. Finding ourselves on the western side of Puget Sound, we were faced with deciding the best route. We could go south and around, but that would take almost an entire day of driving. Factoring in the price of gas, we chose to take the ferry, which proved to be the quickest and most economical way, not to mention the most scenic and interesting. Driving our rig, which was over 50 feet in length onto a ferry was definitely a new experience. From Port Townsend we took the ferry to Coupeville, WA.

We drove over the Deception Pass Bridge and east on Route 20 to the North Cascades National Park. Beautiful aqua lakes and dramatic mountain ranges spread before us. The mountains and pine forest join together in a montage of grays and greens. We are pretty sure that we have seen some of the best that Washington has to offer.

From our new home in the Cascades we did lots of day trips, one of which was to Everett, WA, home of the Boeing plant, to see where all the big planes come from. Boeing is a city within itself. Over 30,000 people work there and the assembly floor space would hold over 800 hockey rinks. Watching a 777 come down the assembly line was pretty impressive, but not as much as the assembly of their new 787. It looks like an airplane but everything about it is different. No aluminum skin, no rivets and the only things with metal in them are some of the control surfaces. The fuselage arrives at the plant in three sections, complete with everything that goes inside it. Basically, they put the sections together, attach the wings and tail section and the plane is ready for rollout in just three and a half days. Pity they don't allow photography inside the plant.

After our tour of the Boeing Plant, we took a short ferry ride over to Whidbey Island, which happens to be one of the longest islands in the United States.

As we left the port we went right past Mukilteo Lighthouse, which is still in operation. After driving the entire length of the island from south to north, we ended up in Anacortes and had a delightful dinner before driving back to our motor home, which was at our new park located in Concrete, WA.

Tacoma lies nestled in Commencement Bay at the bottom of Puget Sound. It is reminiscent of San Francisco a long time ago. Big Brother Seattle is about an hour's drive to the North.

The Museum of Glass is in the historic part of town, across from the old railway station, which is now the county courthouse. The museum, which is more a gallery with a "hot shop", houses current and ongoing exhibitions.

The work of Dale Chihuly is everywhere. A bridge has been built over the train tracks joining the museum and the courthouse, and is appropriately named the "Chihuly Bridge of Glass". Along the bridge is a display called the "Venetian Wall" and it houses dozens of pieces of his early work which was influenced by the Murano glass blowers of Venice. The ceiling of the bridge houses a collage of sea forms in glass, which is backlit by the sun in the daytime and by artificial lighting at night. It is quite a spectacular in any light.

The North Cascades Loop takes you through several National Parks and Forests where you will see everything from volcanic peaks to glacial lakes. This route was not even possible until 1972, when the highway was finished. Even though it was late June, we still found ourselves hiking through snow.

Washington Pass Overlook is the highest point on the North Cascades Highway at 6,477 feet. From here you can see Liberty Bell Mountain, which reaches a height of 7,720 feet in elevation.

View of elusive **Mt. Baker** at sunset as seen from our campsite in Concrete.

This was our last stop before heading North to Canada and beautiful British Columbia.

One of the most spectacular sights along the North Cascades scenic Loop is Diablo Lake. Its amazing jade green color comes from the glacial runoff which contains suspended mineral sediment which refracts the light.

THE CANADIAN ROCKIES

THE CANADIAN ROCKIES

Canada Place

Royal Canadian Mounted Police

Murant's Curve

Although most residents live in high-rise condominiums, some folks still prefer to be closer to sea level, as evidenced by the vast number of houseboats.

Due to the ever-increasing cost of fuel, we decided to leave our motor home in Washington and venture into Canada just by car. We stayed with friends part of the time and took advantage of our timeshares the rest. It worked out very well since you can explore more places by car than with a large rig such as ours.

Our first stop was Vancouver, one of our favorite cities. Here the sea meets the mountains and east meets west in the midst of a modern urban community. From the city center to the Gastown district with its shops and galleries to Granville Island with its wonderful international market and fine restaurants, there is something for all.

Vancouver is one of the great centers for Northwest Native Art and the best examples can be found at Eagle Spirit Gallery on Granville Island, which happens to be where our collection began.

From the city you can easily travel by ferry to the city of Victoria, which is on Vancouver Island. The Ski Resort town of Whistler is just a two and a half hour drive away, via the "Sea-to-Sky Highway". To the northeast is the gateway to the rest of British Columbia and the Canadian Rockies, our next stop.

Canada Place, with its cloth roofing that resembles sails is a landmark which can be seen from all around, including from planes landing or taking off. The complex features hotels, shops, restaurants, and is also where more than 900,000 cruise passengers set sail every year.

Vancouver was the host of the 2010 Winter Olympic Games. You can check out the famous Olympic Torch which has been permanently placed down by the waterfront near Canada Place.

The inukshuk may have been used originally as a point of reference to mark travel routes or spots of interest. It was also the symbol chosen for the 2010 Winter Games and many can be seen around town in various places.

From Vancouver we headed east towards Kelowna, only to be stopped by a mudslide which closed the entire highway. All traffic had to exit and find alternate routes. The Frasier River was raging as were most of the rivers due to the melting snow runoff of the previous season.

Kelowna is located in the Okanagan Valley, which is the agricultural center for most of western Canada as well as their wine country. Because of the climate, this area is the vacation spot for most Canadians. Many even own second homes there, such as our friends with whom we stayed.

We made it to our timeshare resort in Panorama, Alberta, which was just outside of Banff National Park. While there, we relaxed and did day trips to the surrounding sights. One of which was Radium Hot Springs, just one of many hot springs throughout the Canadian Rockies. We spent an entire day there, just relaxing.

While exploring downtown Banff, we discovered the fabulous Cascade Gardens. It was as if a Monet painting had come to life and we were a part of it. As it was getting close to lunch time, we decided why not have a picnic.

After lunch, we visited the famous Banff Springs Hotel. This luxury hotel was one of several grand railway hotels built in the 19th century. It opened to the public in 1888.

Banff National Park is full of spectacular features and natural wonders. From the moment you enter the park, you get up front and personal with the mighty forces of nature which shaped this remarkable and beautiful area, not to mention the many indigenous creatures who call this area home.

Can you even imagine how many years it took for this raging river to form this natural bridge?

The Bow River Valley just outside of Banff. What a spectacular ride it must be on the train which goes right along the banks following its every curve.

The famous Chateau Lake Louise Hotel, which sits on the very edge of the lake, is another one of the remarkable hotels built by the railway in the 19th century.

Lake Louise is almost too perfect to be true. It is nestled between mountains and fed by Victoria Glacier directly behind the lake. Lake Louise is one of the most well-known areas in the Canadian Rockies. It serves as a year-round vacation destination. In addition to attracting summer vacationers, it is also a world class ski area during the winter season.

Just a few miles down the road from Lake Louise is Lake Moraine. Although not as well-known, many feel that Lake Moraine, with its multi-peaked mountains surrounding it, is even more picturesque. We certainly agree with this consensus. Seems like the beauty of the Canadian Rockies just does not stop!

Castle Mountain

Where the Ice Fields begin

The Lodge at Panorama

These are some of the sights we saw on the way to Jasper

Flower Stands at Lake Louise

We headed north towards Jasper, via the Ice Fields Parkway. Due to weather closing in around us, we could not see more than about a third of the lower mountains surrounding us. However, what we were able to see was spectacular!

The Athabasca Glacier, located along the Parkway, is the most visited glacier in North America due to its easy access from the road.

After a 400 mile detour due to yet another road washout, we finally arrived in Prince George, BC to spend a week with friends. They took us up to their cabin on Cluculz Lake, which is just about 45 minutes west of the city. While there, we got plenty of rest and relaxation before having to head south back to the states.

Just like the setting sun says good-bye to the day, we must say good-bye to not only our dear friends, but also to one of the most beautiful places on earth. Now we know why the license plates say "Beautiful BC".

As we approach the United States border, our main concern was getting our parrot, Sam, back into the country. Luckily there was not a problem and we soon found ourselves back in the USA.

So ends part one of our North American Journey. We decided to stay in the Northwest for a while. There is so much to see and do in this part of the country and we need to regroup and rebuild our finances so that we can continue our adventure in the not too distant future.

YELLOWSTONE

Old Faithful

Grand Prismatic Springs

Prarie Bison

On the surface, Yellowstone National Park has beautiful mountains, lush forests, rolling plains, meandering rivers, placid lakes and abundant wildlife. Yet a mere 35 miles below the surface is untold violence. Yellowstone just happens to be the "hottest" spot on our planet. Thanks to the many springs and underground water sources, this molten mass that lies beneath the ground is kept in check, at least for now.

The smell of sulphur seems to dominate the air and everywhere we went the ground appeared to be bubbling and boiling all around us. It was if the park itself was alive.

Little Geyser near Old Faithful

Grand Prismatic Springs

Blue Spring

Purple Mountains and spacious skies above Yellowstone's plain.

Mule Deer

Elk

Gibbon Falls

The Yellowstone River runs through the park and at every turn there is more extraordinary scenery.

Of course one cannot go to Yellowstone without making a pilgrimage to Old Faithful. It can take up to 2 hours for the pressure to build before erupting for a mere 1-5 minutes. But as we discovered, people don't mind the wait. We have to agree with them – it is well worth it!

Inland from the lake are the vast plains and the local buffalo (bison) herd, whose favorite pastime is blocking the road out of Canyon Village. Everywhere we went we had to go through this area, which we so lovingly referred to as "Buffalo Alley". They would come right up to our car. We could literally reach out and touch them. But we didn't.

Little Grand Canyon Upper Falls

We spent our last day in the northwest corner of the park in an area called Mammoth Hot Springs. We were a bit misled by the name and were hoping for a "soak". But it was not that sort of hot springs. We did, however get to go horseback riding, where we were able to see some of the quieter areas of the park.

Little Fire Hole River

As the day quietly comes to an end, we must prepare to move on. Yellowstone has truly been an exciting stop on our journey through North America. Perhaps one day we shall return.

In the southeastern corner of Idaho lies an alien landscape known as Craters of the Moon National Monument. In fact, it is so alien that NASA chose it as a training site for our Apollo Astronauts in preparation for the future moon landings.

The entire area is a massive lava flow from multiple volcanic eruptions dating back over 15,000 years ago, the most recent being just 2000 years ago. The park covers 1,117 square miles and contains everything from lava flows to vents and cinder cones with the volcanic mountains always on the horizon.

A nice treat was the variety of wild flowers that sprung up just about everywhere.

The Grand Tetons as seen across Jenny Lake

Jenny Lake wildlife

Taggert Lake

This is a view from Antelope Flats. But one of our favorite vantage spots was from the Jackson Lake Lodge. Where else could you get an incredible view and a lobster roll with your beer?

Last Stand Hill

Where they fell

The Little Big Horn Valley lies in what is now southern Montana. Here the northern Cheyenne joined with the Hunkpapa Sioux under the leadership of Sitting Bull, a revered medicine man and spiritual leader. Other tribes joined including the Oglala Sioux, led by Crazy Horse, a fierce and determined warrior and war chief. In all, some 7,000 Indians were camped along the Little Big Horn River. Over 1200 to 1500 of them were warriors, well-armed and ready for battle, all with the same goal of refusing to be herded into reservations away from their traditional lands and hunting grounds. They simply refused to give up their way of life.

Custer led five companies of 40-50 men each, totaling 221 troops into the valley. Behind him was Capt. Benteen with 120 troops and Lt. Reno with 175 more. Rather than remain as a unified force, Custer split his men into three groups and ran headlong into the overwhelming Indian force. This was his second fatal mistake. His first being that he under estimated the number of braves he was facing. Nor could he conceive of the Indians working together as a unified and well-organized fighting force.

The Indians' attack plan was simple, a buffalo hunt. Custer and all of his men were lost in that terrible battle. They really never had a chance. Benteen and Reno could only watch in horror from their positions above the Indian encampment. They too were under attack and Reno had lost almost half of his men retreating to high ground.

This is a peaceful place today, except for the white and red markers which show where brave soldiers and Indians fell.

The vibrations are still here.

Indian encampment on the Little Big Horn, as seen from Reno's high ground

Some of the markers

Devil's Tower National Monument, located in Wyoming, stands over 5,000 feet high in the middle of nowhere like an apparition. At first sight, it appears as if it were somehow placed there, however the mystery of how it was formed has yet to be solved. It is a sacred place to the local tribes and offerings can be found in the trees scattered around the monument.

There is a wonderful hiking trail going completely around the base, where you can see in greater detail the columnar rock formations which make up this sculpture in stone. On any given day climbers can be seen working their way to the top plateau of this massive rock.

We camped in its massive shadow and could not help but remember that well-known movie by Steven Spielberg from 1977, "Close Encounters of the Third Kind".

Today, the only aliens that call this place home are the black-tailed prairie dogs that live in the grounds near the entrance to the park.

One of the most famous landmarks in South Dakota is Mt. Rushmore. It is a symbol of our country and democracy. Carved out of the granite of South Dakota's Black Hills, it stands as a lasting memorial to our founding fathers and visionary leaders.

The area around the monument is filled with lakes, streams and mountain vistas.

About 30 miles from Rushmore is the still unfinished monument to Chief Crazy Horse, leader of the Lakota Oglala Sioux, who was looked on as a great chief and inspiration to his people. This work is being completed by surviving members of the Borglum family who were also responsible for nearby Mt. Rushmore and Stone Mountain, near Atlanta GA.

Mountain goats as well as many other animals can be found throughout this area. Guess they like it here as well.

The skies are truly beautiful and provide the most glorious sunsets you could ever imagine.

South Dakota is a land of rich forests, beautiful lakes, hard granite mountains and soft rolling prairies. These prairies are almost as hypnotic as the sea.

The hills are often referred to as the "Black Hills" of South Dakota, so named for their dense vegetation, which seen from a distance makes them appear black.

Wall, South Dakota is home of the most famous drugstore in America, Wall Drug. Started in the thirties and made famous by a simple glass of ice water, it is now a national institution and famous the world over. You've heard of a "one horse town"? Well, this is a "one store town". If you are looking for anything western or otherwise, you will find it there. Yes, it is still a pharmacy as well. Neat store……

Approximately 26,000 years ago when mammoths roamed the American northwest, a sinkhole opened up just south of what is now Rapid City, SD. Over 60 of these creatures walked, or fell in and could not get themselves out. Their fossilized remains are being painstakingly uncovered at this site. Here the seemingly random collection of Pleistocene bones is making sense to the many paleontologists who come here from all over the world to work.

Welcome to the Badlands National Park of South Dakota. To the Lakota Sioux this land was called "Mako Sica". The French trappers called it "Les Mauvaises Terres". They both translate loosely to mean "Bad Land".

This unique landscape was created about 500,000 years ago and to this day is ever changing due to wind and water erosion. The park covers over 244,000 acres.

Imagine being a 19th century pioneer headed west to find a new home. You are gently crossing the peaceful Dakota prairies, when all of a sudden the world ends! Before you are miles of an eaten away landscape that you and your wagons are unable to cross. No trees, no grasses, no water and no end in sight.

The most famous landmark in the Colorado Springs area is Pikes Peak, the most visited mountain in North America. Although some hiked up to the 14,115 foot peak, we chose to drive. Even the drive up was slow and tedious with its many hairpin turns with steep drop-offs just inches away from our tires, not to mention the many bicyclists all over the place. We made it to the summit, which was quite barren and housed only a ranger station and a gift shop. But the views were quite spectacular and we felt like we could literally kiss the clouds. We did not stay long, due to the high altitude and lack of oxygen. The drive down was just as tedious as the drive up. About midway down the mountain the Park Rangers stop you and check your brakes for over-heating. Most everyone is required to pull over for a few minutes before continuing their journey to the bottom.

Not far from Pikes Peak, we found the little frontier town of Cripple Creek. Not the one made famous by The Band. That one is in the Carolinas. This one was a pretty typical western town except that behind almost every store-front was a casino. So much for preserving history.

Southwest of Colorado Springs and just above the New Mexico border is the small town of Antonito. We stayed just outside of this small community. Not much there except for the mountains, valleys and the Conejos River.

We discovered that they obviously must have pretty liberal building codes, judging by this house we saw in town. We heard a couple of different stories about the guy who lives there. But we will let the picture speak for itself.

The very peaceful Conejos River

Just down the road from Antonito and over the 10,022 foot Cumbres Pass and into New Mexico is the town of Chama, home of the Cumbres & Toltec Scenic Railroad. It is one of the few remaining narrow gauge coal fired steam railroads in America today. The run is from Chama to Antonito and goes over that 10,000 ft. pass. How they keep these antique trains with their 90 year old engines running is a wonder. The ride was scenic and great fun, but also quite sooty. The open range laws give the cows the right of way, so our journey was interrupted on several occasions when the cows decided to occupy the tracks. This reminded us a little of the buffalo back in Yellowstone.

THE SOUTHEAST

The Ozark National Forest in Arkansas is lush, green and full of life. Pedestal Rocks is an area of huge rock formations carved out by ancient rivers. The hiking trail ends where they begin.

Further into the forest is a formation known as the "Natural Bridge", also carved by water and quite majestic, especially when viewed from below.

Hot Springs National Park is also in Arkansas and is the smallest of all the National Parks. In many ways, this is our "oldest" National Park. Back in 1832, 40 years before Yellowstone became the first National Park, President Andrew Jackson set aside the hot springs as a special reservation. However it did not officially become a National Park until 1921.

This park is also unique in that it borders the town of the same name. The town prospered in the mid-19th century as a health spa and attracted those seeking relief from many health issues.

In the heart of the park is "Bathhouse Row" featuring elegant spas, some of which still operate today.

Each day about 700,000 gallons of water (143 degrees F) flow from the springs into the reservoir system and is channeled to the bathhouses.

The row of bathhouses is connected by the Grand Promenade, a brick walkway that took 30 years to build and landscape.

Following down the Nimrod River we came upon a TVA dam. A nice little piece of engineering.

Hiking trails abound throughout the area. Many trails can be accessed right from the Grand Promenade. Be sure to keep an eye out for some of the locals.

We couldn't go to Memphis without seeing where Elvis lived. Graceland was not at all what we expected. There is nothing pretentious about this house; no silver candelabras, no gold faucets and no million dollar paintings on the walls. Just a very nice home built for relaxing and entertaining friends. The only glitz was in the costumes that he wore. Everything in the interior says "Hey, come on in, take a load off".

The house is about music. There is something to play on everywhere, every room a potential jam session.

Some of the space has been converted into galleries in order to display his almost countless awards. Just about every song he sang won something.

Outside the house is a simple backyard and pool area which is also where Elvis and his parents are laid to rest. Such a simple gravesite. Adjacent to this area is a small pasture surrounded by trees. Totally lovely and totally peaceful. To us, this speaks volumes about Mr. Elvis Presley.

We stayed at an RV park on the Arkansas side right on the Mississippi River. During the day we would watch the bustling barge and riverboat traffic, but as the evening neared, you would find us across the river in Memphis, Tennessee, "Home of the Blues".

What most people don't realize is that before the big record labels took over, the industry, there was Sun and Stax Records, which ushered in Rock and Roll and brought the blues to life and out to the public. Sadly, both of these labels are gone, but the music is still with us.

Beale Street is where it's at! It is so alive! The music is everywhere and the Mecca seems to be at BB King's Blues Club, where we spent several nights. And did we mention the food? We enjoyed everything from seafood to barbecue. All of it great!

We got to the Great Smoky Mountains National Park just as the Government Shutdown of 2013 went into effect. It's just not right when you have to break the law to see some of our national treasures.

The Smoky Mountains are also some of the oldest mountains on earth. They got their name because the evaporation of moisture which builds up on the leaves of the trees and vegetation creates a "smoky haze" as it mixes with the air.

These lush mountains and valleys are a treat to behold and seem to go on forever. This was very different from the rugged and rocky landscapes of the Rockies. There is a great gentleness about this area.

There are over 800 miles of hiking trails throughout the Great Smoky Mountains. Just about all of the trails and view areas were blocked off by the government, but that did not stop us or lots of other folks wo came to enjoy what is normally the nation's busiest park. We hiked where we could and saw what we could.

One of the most popular and spectacular seasons to visit this area is the fall, when the leaves are changing to the brilliant colors of the season. We were just a little too early to catch the full explosion of colors, but we did see the beginning of the transition from summer to fall. Some of the hiking trails followed rippling streams and as the light shone through the trees it illuminated the falling leaves as if they were flecks of gold falling from the sky.

The U.S. Space and Rocket Center in Huntsville, AL helped pioneer our space program and our journey to the moon. Begun in 1960, it became the home of Werner Von Braun and his team of German rocket scientists. Here is where he helped create the massive rocket engines that would propel us to the moon.

Apollo 16 Command Module

The Saturn V's first stage engine, the now famous F-1, is one of the most powerful ever built. The Russians had developed a stronger one, but unfortunately theirs all blew up at launch, which ended their N-1 manned lunar program.

Today a new breed of young rocket scientists and engineers are working to re-develop the F-1 and have even raided the Smithsonian as well as other air and space museums for parts and insight. Our new program is called "Orion" and is multi-purpose and involves a partially reusable spacecraft that combines the technologies from both the Apollo and Space Shuttle programs.

They also conduct "Space Camp" programs for kids and adults. It is a one-week course with hands-on training in the field of science and space-age technology.

The new Space Launch System which when combined with the Orion Spacecraft will take Astronauts further into space than ever before.

Apollo Saturn first stage F-1 rocket engines

Our home base when we started out was at Styx River, located in Robertsdale, AL, just across the state line form Pensacola, FL and a few miles from Mobile. This location gave us the opportunity to visit several nearby sights.

Not many know this, but Mardi Gras actually began in Mobile, AL back in 1703, fifteen years before New Orleans was enen founded. Mardi Gras is the oldest annual carnival celebration in the United States. While there we visited the Mobile Mardi Gras Museum, where you can see examples of the elaborate costumes and other memorabilia from past years.

In contrast to the colorful costumes of Mardi Gras is Battleship Memorial Park, which is home to the USS Alabama. Commissioned in 1942, it was the sixth to ever bear the name "Alabama". After the war, she was no longer needed and was decommissioned on January 9, 1947 and placed on reserve duty. She was retired in 1962 and in 1964 taken to Mobile Bay and opened the following year as a museum ship. The USS Alabama was added to the National Historic Landmark registry in 1986.

GEORGIA

GEORGIA

Tybee Island Light House

Rock City

When Sherleen was a young girl, she and her family visited Rock City while on a family camping trip along the Blue Ridge Parkway. Rock City and nearby Ruby Falls are located at Lookout Mountain, GA, not far from Chattanooga, TN.

Rock City is a natural formation of huge boulders atop Lookout Mountain. From the summit on an outcropping called "Lovers Leap" and on a clear day, seven states can be seen.

Coleus and moss adding colors to nature's palette

The area was developed as a public attraction beginning in 1924 by the Carter family. Using a string, Frieda Carter laid out what would become the pathways in and around the formations. Plantings were added throughout, and in 1932 Rock City Gardens was officially opened to the public, with what was rather a weak response. Nobody knew where or what it was. Then along came a sign painter named Clark Byers who created an ad campaign by painting barns around the country. The deal was that he would paint your barn in exchange for letting him add three words to the side or roof. "SEE ROCK CITY". Well, it worked and Rock City has been popular ever since. There are even a few of those barns still standing and still legible.

Chattanooga, TN can be seen in the background from atop Lookout Mountain

Fall colors. Some placed there by Mother Nature, while others were not. Both adding to the spirit of this colorful time of the year.

Stone Bridge

One of the famous "Rock City" Bird Houses

Not too far down the road from Rock City and deep inside Lookout Mountain lies another natural wonder, Ruby Falls. This underground phenomenon was discovered in 1928 by Leo Lambert and a few adventurous friends as they crawled their way deep into the caverns toward the sound of rushing water. At about 1000 feet below the surface they came upon a chamber with a mysterious 145 foot waterfall. Leo named it after his wife, Ruby. To this day, no one is exactly certain where the source for this amazing waterfall is.

You descend down to the cave floor via an elevator and make your way through the winding corridors of the cave, where you are surrounded by incredible limestone formations. At the end of the corridor you enter a large cavern and stand waiting in the dark for the music to start and the lights to come up. All of a sudden you are looking up at one of the most incredible sights you could ever imagine. There before you is Ruby Falls.

Okefenokee
Swamp
Park
WAYCROSS, GEORGIA

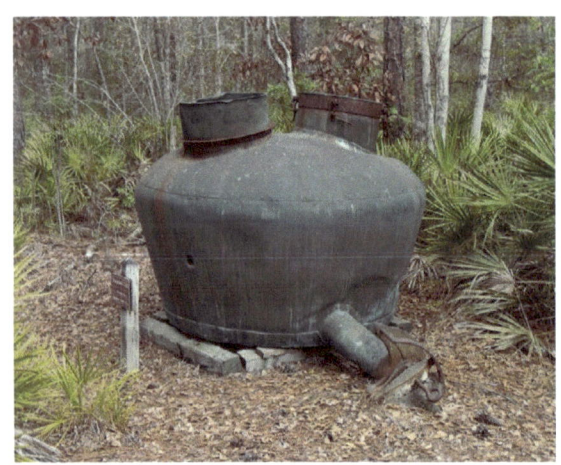

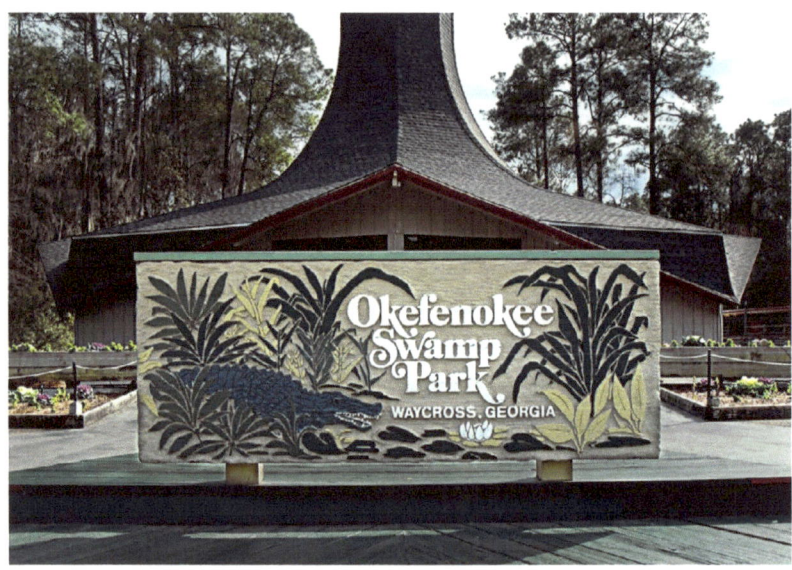

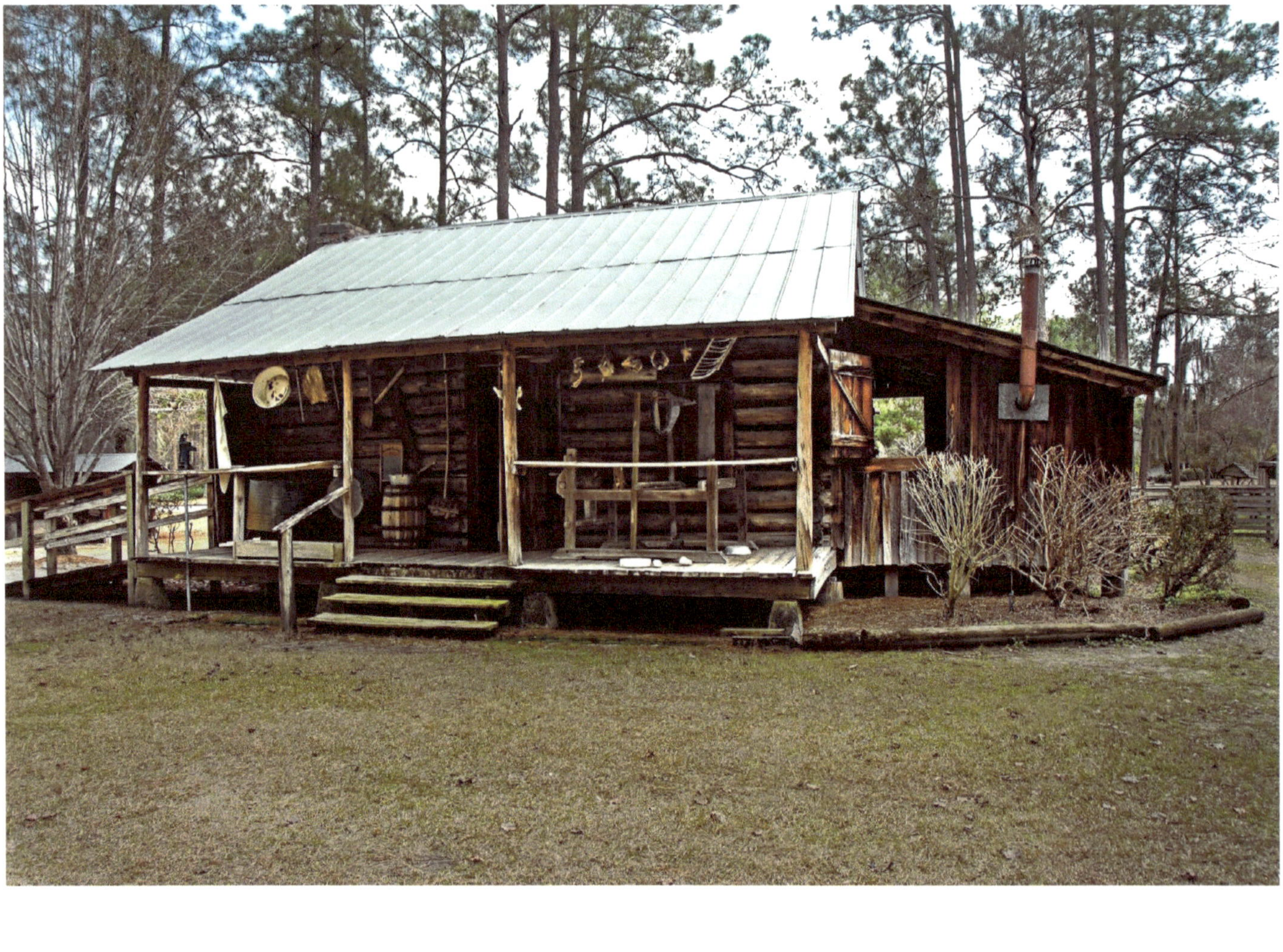

The Okefenokee Swamp, located in southern Georgia, is home to a variety of wildlife, especially alligators. But the real treat here, is their homage to Walt Kelly. This is where all of his characters came from and we think where some of his heart was.

One of the most popular characters that called Okefenokee home was "Pogo" the possum, who has been around since 1943.

Just outside of Savannah, GA is another one of our favorite places. Every time that we are there we always have to eat at "The Crab Shack" on Tybee Island. In addition to the great seafood, we enjoy the setting, right on the bay. The tables have holes in the center, so as you eat, you discard any shells or bones by pushing them forward and into the hole, where a garbage can is strategically placed. No mess, no fuss.

Situated between Tybee Island and Savannah, GA is the Fort Pulaski National Monument. Construction on the fort began in 1829 and took 18 years to complete. At the time it was considered "invincible" and as strong as the Rocky Mountains. The walls were made of solid brick, 7 ½ feet thick and backed with massive masonry piers. But even with all of that, it could not withstand the heavy impact of rifled artillery of heavy caliber.

On April 10th, 1862, the Union opened fire on the fort and after just 30 hours of battle, the fortress was breached and surrendered to the Union.

THE CAROLINAS

Kitty Hawk

St Michael's Church, Charleston, S.C.

The Biltmore Estate

THE CAROLINAS

Port Washington, South Carolina

Ashville, NC is a city that somehow seems out of place in the deep South. It is more like a town outside of Boston or Seattle, with its feeling and attitude. There are lots of galleries, bookstores, theatres and sidewalk cafes and good music everywhere.

The Grove Park Inn and the Biltmore Estate are two of the most well-known landmarks in Ashville. The Grove Park Inn was built by Edwin Grove, a pharmacist turned millionaire when he created a magic elixir that was sold throughout the country. Building began in 1910 and took less than a year to complete, using 400 craftsmen working six ten-hour shifts per week. The fact that they were paid well helped speed things along. Today it is one of the highest ranked hotels in the country. What a joy it was simply to walk through this magnificent place.

The view from the back deck of the Grove Park Inn

The Biltmore Estate took a little longer to build than the Grove Hotel. Construction began in 1888 by George Vanderbilt and was completed in time for the Vanderbilt Christmas party of 1895, which would be the first of many such extravaganzas. The Vanderbilt family loved to entertain, especially Mrs. Vanderbilt. The mansion, which is the largest single family residence in the United States, consists of 255 rooms and 175,000 square feet of interior space. The entire estate covers many square miles and it would have taken a week to ride around the property on horseback.

Richard Morris Hunt was the chief architect and Frederick Law Olmstead was the landscape designer. Mr. Olmstead was also the landscape designer for New York's Central Park and in his spare time he also managed to design and build the base for the Statue of Liberty in New York Harbor.

Sadly, George Vanderbilt did not live long enough to fully enjoy the estate. He died in 1914 at the early age of 52. The estate is palatial and filled with artistic gems from all over the world. The John Singer Sargent portraits in the grand dining room were especially impressive. The grounds and the gardens are also magnificent and inviting. If visiting, plan to spend the entire day. There is a lot to see and enjoy.

More views of the Biltmore Estate

From the Pacific to the Atlantic. We made it!

The Atlantic coast is very different from the northwest coast. Not as picturesque, but more inviting, and of course, much warmer.

The Cape Hatteras Lighthouse can be seen in the distance. This was as close as we could get to the Outer Banks of North Carolina, due to the government shut down.

We did get to see Kitty Hawk, sort of, by walking in past the barriers. Although the Visitor Center and Museum were closed, also due to government shut down, we were able to roam around the outside of the park. While there, we met other visitors who shared our determination. Some had come all the way from Europe to see our country and its sights. The park seems very understated for such an important moment in our history. We do know why the Wright brothers chose this particular sight for their first flight. It is quiet, flat and has steady ocean breezes.

The bronze replica near the monument commemorates the importance of what took place on and above this ground.

One of our last stops was in Myrtle Beach, SC. Even in October there were still lots of people enjoying the sunshine and beaches.

We did a day trip to nearby Charleston. What a wonderful city. The streets are lined with elegant homes dating back hundreds of years. In the center of town is the Straw Market, which is one of the oldest public facilities with continuous use in the country.

One of the prominent landmarks is the historical St. Michael's Church, the oldest surviving religious structure in Charleston.

Preceeding page: Waterfront Park, Charleston, SC.

Our campsite in Myrtle Beach was right on the Intracoastal Waterway, and as we watched the boats cruise by, we started thinking about our next journey. Perhaps trading our wheels for a keel? But for now, we shall return to Florida, where our North American Journey began.

Natural Treasures

We visited 21 of the lower 48 states during our journey across North America, along with two Canadian provinces. We feel very fortunate to have seen some of the most beautiful and treasured sights that both countries have to offer.

National Parks and Monuments

Gulf Islands National Seashore, FL
Castillo de San Marcos, FL
Jean Lafitte National Historical Park & Preserve, LA
Yosemite National Park, CA
Mt. St. Helens National Volcanic Monument, WA
Mt. Rainier National Park, WA
Olympic National Park, WA
North Cascades National Park, WA
Crater Lake National Park, OR
Newberry National Volcanic Monument, OR
Craters of the Moon National Monument & Preserve, ID
Yellowstone National Park, WY
Grand Teton National Park, WY
Little Bighorn Battlefield National Monument, MT
Devil's Tower National Monument, WY
Mt. Rushmore National Memorial, SD
Badlands National Park, SD
Pikes Peak National Forest, CO
Ozark National Forest, AR
Hot Springs National Park, AR
Great Smoky Mountains National Park, TN
Blue Ridge Parkway, NC
Wright Brothers National Memorial, NC
Fort Pulaski National Monument, GA

State Parks

Stephen Foster Folk Culture Center State Park, FL
Homosassa Springs Wildlife State Park, FL
Yulee Sugar Mill Ruins Historic State Park, FL
Blue Spring State Park, FL
Bulow Plantation Ruins Historic State Park, FL
Florida Caverns State Park, FL
Dinosaur Valley State Park, TX
Shasta State Historic Park, CA
Umpqua Lighthouse State Park, OR
Devils Punchbowl State Park, OR
Cape Kiwanda State Park, OR
Cape Lookout State Park, OR
Cape Meares State Park, OR

National Wildlife Refuges

Okeefenokee National Wildlife Refuge, GA
Dungeness National Wildlife Refuge, WA
Flattery Rocks National Wildlife Refuge, WA
Sequim National Wildlife Refuge, WA

National Wildlife Refuges

Banff National Park, Alberta, CA

Just the Facts

Our home on wheels consumed 1,813 gallons of fuel during our journey, at a cost of $6,728.48. When we began our trip gas was selling for $2.99 per gallon and by the time we reached California it peaked at $4.31 per gallon. By the end of our journey it was back down to $3.10 per gallon. We averaged just 6.37 mpg, thus making fuel our largest road trip expense.

In additional to the gas for the motor home. We spent an additional $2,016.66 on gas for our car, which we used for touring nearby sights.

During our 339 nights on the road, we stayed at:

58 RV parks
1 state park
4 National Parks
6 Walmarts
1 Home Depot
1 Camping World
and 1 auto garage.

Our overall camping fees totaled $5,871.03, making our average per night cost just $17.32.

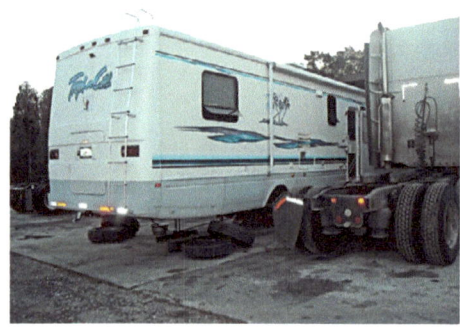

We spent $5,956.29 on repairs and maintenance while on the road., which included new brakes, new tires, montorhome batteries, generator and tow dolly repairs.

Other items worth noting

Miles driven: 13,171

Groceries: $4341.49

Laundry: $98.25

Sightseeing: $655.61